D0524694

ICELAND

SO QUIET

ICELAND SO QUIET
Photographs: © Kristján Ingi Einarsson
www.kristjaningi.is
Text: © Ari Trausti Guðmundsson
Translation: Keneva Kunz
Cover design: Rósa Hrund Kristjánsdóttir
Layout: Kristján Ingi Einarsson

First printing, March 2010
Second printing, May 2011
Printed in China: Prentmidlun Ltd.
ISBN 978-9935-418-25-8
SALKA – REYKJAVÍK – 2011

Cover photo: The craters Nyrðri-Eldborg and Syðri-Eldborg, Svínahraun lava flow.

ICELAND
SO QUIET

KRISTJÁN INGI EINARSSON
www.salka.is

Alpine mouse ear

The fissure Flosagjá on the plains of Þingvellir

Lake Mývatn, in North Iceland

Glacial lagoon Jökulsárlón and Öræfajökull, a glacier-topped volcano

Mud cracks

Volcanic tuff outcrop on Helgafell, Southwest Iceland

Svörtuloft, on The Snæfellsnes peninsula

A mineral spring, Ölkelda, on The Snæfellsnes peninsula

Puffin

Cliffs at Látrabjarg, on the westernmost extremity of Europe

Peaks of Hraundrangar, above the farm Hraun in Öxnadalur

Two of the Westman Islands, Elliðaey and Bjarnarey, and the glacier-capped volcano Eyjafjallajökull

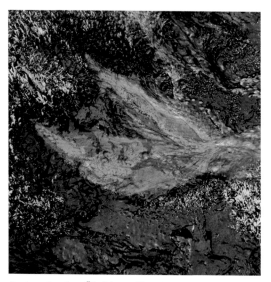

A mineral spring, Ölkelda, on The Snæfellsnes peninsula

Aurora borealis – Northern lights

The glacial tongue of The Skaftafellsjökull

Island of Sandey in Lake Þingvallavatn

Cotton grass

Lava formations of Dimmuborgir, near Lake Mývatn in North Iceland

The glacial lagoon Jökulsárlón

Skinnalón on Melrakkaslétta, on the northeast edge of Iceland

Cormorants

Outcrops at Skálasnagi, on The Snæfellsnes peninsula

Landmannalaugar, in South Central Iceland

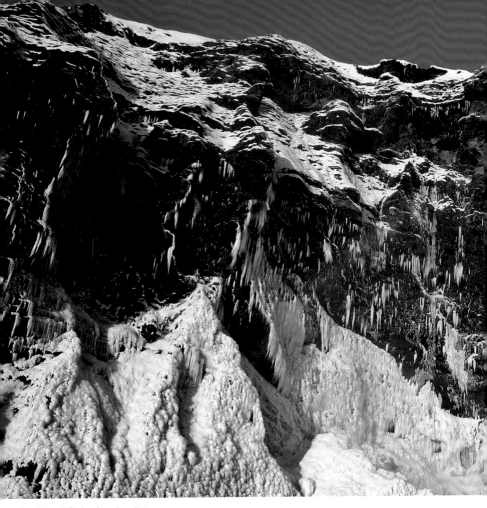

The falls of Skógafoss in winter

Mountain avens

Ernir, on The Snæfellsnes peninsula

Black sand beaches at Héraðssandur, East Iceland

Lyme grass in Vöðlavík in the East Fjords

Buttercup

Hólaskjól, in South Central Iceland

The glacier atop the volcano Snæfellsjökull

Ásbyrgi, in Northeast Iceland

Snow-topped hillocks

The mountain Keilir on The Reykjanes peninsula

Hraunlandarif and Grafarós, on The Snæfellsnes peninsula

A peak of Rauðufossafjöll with the red falls from which it takes its name

Snowflower

The peak Hnappur on the glacier topping the volcano Öræfajökull

Gullfoss, the Golden Falls

The geysir Strokkur about to erupt

Strokkur in full flight, in Haukadalur, South Iceland

On the glacier Sólheimajökull

Arnarfjörður, in the West Fjords

Peaks of Jarlhettur in the background

Valley of Ólafsdalur, in Gilsfjörður, West Iceland

Hraunlandarif, on The Snæfellsnes peninsula, with the glacier-topped volcano Snæfellsjökull

The crater Ljótipollur in South Central Iceland

Whimbrel

Grass- and moss-covered lava formations

The mountains Dyrfjöll in the East Fjords

Thermal areas in the mountains Kerlingarfjöll, in Central Iceland

Angelica

The falls Goðafoss on the river Skjálfandafljót in North Iceland

Iceland's most infamous volcano, Mount Hekla, in South Iceland

The cove Harðbaksvík on Melrakkaslétta, at the northeast edge of Iceland

Whooper swan

Álftavatn, or Swan Lake

River Tungnaá, the peak Hamarinn and ice cap Vatnajökull in the distance

Reyðarfjörður, in the East Fjords

Moss campion

Hafrahvammagljúfur by Kárahnjúkar

Lake Álftavatn and the mountain Ingólfsfjall

Northern lights and light column of the Imagine Peace Tower in Reykjavík, from Álftavatn

Dandelions

The waterfall Dynjandi in the West Fjords

Jökulgil in Landmannalaugar, Central Iceland

Geothermal areas at Námaskarð near Lake Mývatn, North Iceland

Puffin

Westman Islands, off the south coast

The mountain Hrafnabjörg, on the plains of Þingvellir

Fjallabak, in the interior highlands

Arctic tern

Barðsneshorn, the easternmost point of mainland Iceland

Sprengisandur and the ice cap Hofsjökull

The beach Reynisfjara and Dyrhólaey, south coast

Ptarmigan in summer

The glacier topping the volcano Snæfellsjökull

Arnarfjörður, in the West Fjords

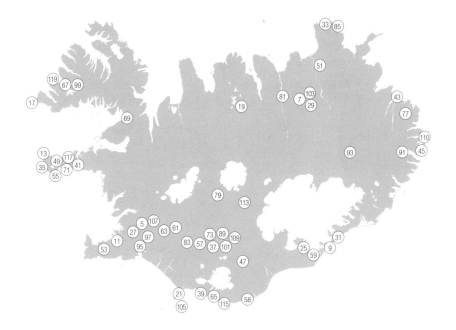